The Hip Hope Dancer

Written & Illustrated by
the Grade 7 & 8 Class of Quluaq School

Edited by
Dawn Elizabeth Doyle

The Hip Hope Dancer

Published by ***The Reading DEN***
1267 Canal Road, Brechin, ON, L0K 1B0

www.dawnofcompositon.vpweb.ca

Library and Archives Canada Cataloguing in Publication

The hip hope dancer / written & illustrated by the Grade 7 & 8 class of Quluaq School ; edited by Dawn Elizabeth Doyle. -- Third edition.

Issued also in electronic format.
Text in English and in Inuktitut.
ISBN 978-0-9959273-0-8 (softcover).--ISBN 978-0-9959273-1-5 (HTML)

1. School prose, Canadian--Nunavut--Clyde River. 2. Children's writings, Canadian--Nunavut--Clyde River. 3. Inuit literature--Canada. 4. Canadian literature (English)--Inuit authors. 5. Quluaq School (Clyde River, Nunavut).I. Doyle, Dawn Elizabeth, editor II. Quluaq School (Clyde River, Nunavut), author

PS8600.H57 2017 jC813'.6 C2017-901899-X
C2017-901900-7

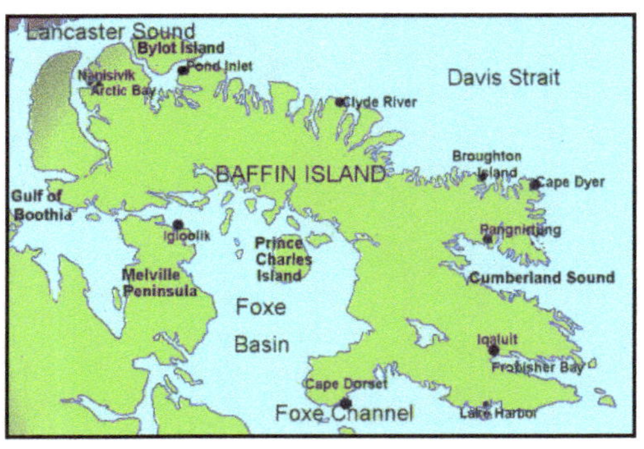

CREDITS

This book is the product of some wonderful teamwork by some very talented Inuit students at Quluaq School in Clyde River, Baffin Island, Nunavut, Canada.

Contributors: 2007-08 Grade 7 & 8 Class

Dina Atagootak
Alisha Atsiqtaq
Lee Anne Hainnu
Joanne Palituq (illustrator)
Jody Palluq (illustrator)
Gina Paniloo
Joseph Primeau
Kareen Qayaq

Grade 12 Mentor

Benny Sanguya

- Coordinated, supervised & edited by English teacher, Dawn Elizabeth Doyle
- Technical assistance by computer teacher, Geoffy Ivany
- Many thanks to their Inuktitut translator, Jennifer Jaypoody
- A special thanks to Meeka Paniloo, their hip hop instructor
- Last, but not least, we want to thank the members of CFM (Canadian Floor Masters) for their inspiration & encouragement to the youth of Clyde River

Canadian Floor Masters

Once upon a modern time, in a little hamlet on Baffin Island, there lived a boy who loved to dance.

His father was one of the best drum dancers in town and so was his grandfather before him.

His name was Isapee. Like his ancestors, he wanted to be a good dancer—but he did not want to drum dance.

He wanted to "*hip hop*" dance!

He had seen hip hop dancers on television and videos and he liked their style, their music and their baggy clothes.

ᐅᐊᑦᑎᐊᕈ, ᓄᓇᓕᕋᑖᑯᓗᖕᓂ ᕿᑭᖅᑖᓗᖕᒥᑦ, ᐊᖑᑎᑕᖅᑲᓗᐅᖅᐳᖅ ᒧᒥᕈᒻᒫᓗᖕᒥᑦ.

ᐊᑖᑕᖓ ᕿᓚᐅᔾᔭᒃᑲᐅᓂᖅᐹᖑᓚᐅᖅᐳᖅ ᓄᓇᓕᖕᓂ ᐊᒻᒪᓗ ᐃᑦᑐᖓ ᐃᓅᓚᐅᖅᑎᓐᓇᒍ.

ᐊᖑᑦ ᑖᓐᓇ ᐊᑎᖅᑲᖅᑐᓂ ᐃᓴᐱᒥᒃ. ᓯᕗᓕᖏᑎᑐᑦ, ᒧᒥᒃᑲᐅᔪᒪᓚᐅᖅᑐᖅ.

ᑭᓯᐊᓂ ᕿᓚᐅᔾᔭᖅᑎᐅᔪᒪᓚᐅᖏᑦᑐᖅ.

Hᐃᑉ Hᐊᑉᑎᐅᖔᕈᒪᓚᐅᖅᑐᕐᓕ!

ᑕᑯᓯᒪᖕᒪᑦ Hᐃᑉ Hᐊᑉ ᒧᒥᖅᑎᓂᒃ ᑏᕖᒃᑯᑦ ᐊᒻᒪᓗ ᑕᕐᕆᔭᐅᑎᒃᑯᑦ ᐊᒻᒪᓗ ᐱᐅᒥᓪᓗᓂᒥᑦ ᒧᒥᐅᓯᖕᒥᑦ, ᑐᓴᕋᓐᓈᕆᖕᒥᑦ ᐊᒻᒪᓗ ᓂᕈᑐᔪᑦ ᐊᓐᓄᕌᖕᒥᑦ.

One day, Canadian Floor Masters came to his hamlet of Clyde River to teach kids how to break dance.

They were flying from town to town to see who was interested in learning how to "*hip hop*".

They organized supervisors in each town to encourage youth to meet three times a week and practice.

ᐅᑦᓗᖅ ᐊᑕᐅᓯᖅ, ᑲᓇᑕᒥᑦ ᒧᒥᖅᑎᓪᒪᓈᑦ ᑎᑭᓪᓚᑕ ᑲᖕᒋᖅᑐᒑᐱᖕᒧᑦ

ᐊᔪᕆᖅᓯᐅᔾᔨᔭᖅᑐᖅᑐᑎᒃ ᓱᕈᓯᕐᓂ ᒧᒥᕆᐅᖅᓴᓂᕐᒥᑦ. ᖃᖕᒐᑕᑲᑕᒃᑐᑎᒃ ᓄᓇᓕᖕᓂ

ᓄᓇᓕᖕᓄᑦ ᖃᐅᔨᓇᓱᒃᑐᑎᒃ ᑭᒃᑯᑦ ᒧᒥᕆᐅᖅᓴᖃᑦᑕᕈᒪᖕᒫᖕᒐᑕ "ᕼᐃᑉ ᕼᐋᑉᒥ."

ᐱᕙᕇᔭᐃᑦᑐᑎᒃ ᖃᐅᔨᓴᖅᑎᒃᓴᓂᒃ ᓄᓇᓕᖕᓂ ᐊᔭᐅᕆᒥᐊᒃᑲᓐᓂᖅᑐᑎᒃ ᒪᒃᑯᒃᑐᓂᒃ

ᑲᑎᖃᑦᑕᕐᑐᑎᒃ ᐱᓇᓱᐊᕈᓯᖅ ᐱᖕᒐᓱᐊᖅᑎᕐᑐᑎᒃ ᐱᔭᕆᐅᖅᓴᕙᓪᓗᑎᒃ.

ᐃᓴᐱ ᐱᖅᑕᐅᕐᑯᔭᐅᑦᑐᓂ ᐊᒻᒪᓗ ᐊᒻᒪᓗ ᐱᔭᕆᐅᖅᓴᕙᒃᑐᓂ ᖃᐅᑕᒫᑦ.

CFM
CFM

But Isapee had a problem.

Each time he practiced "*hip hop*" dancing, he couldn't finish a dance. He always fell down, too tired to finish.

He decided to go around the hamlet and ask for advice.

First he went to his parents and he showed them his "*head spin*" dance. They clapped and clapped—when suddenly he fell down tired. He couldn't finish the dance.

"What have you been doing?" they said. "Better luck next time."

ᑭᓯᐊᓂ ᐃᓴᐱ ᐊᑲᐅᖏᓕᐅᕈᑎᖃᓚᐅᖅᐳᖅ. ᐱᔭᕆᐅᖅᓴᓂᖅᑕᒫᑦ "ᕼᐃᑉ ᕼᐋᑉᒥ" ᒧᒥᕐᓂᕐᒥ ᐱᔭᕇᖅᓯᕙᓐᓇᕐᓇᓂ ᒧᒥᕐᓂᕐᒥ. ᐋᓪᓚᐅᔭᐃᓐᓇᖅᑐᓂ, ᑕᖅᑲᑐᐊᖅᐸᒃᑐᓂᑐ ᐱᔭᕇᖅᓯᔭᕆᐊᒃᓴᖅ.

ᔪᓇᓕᖕᓂ ᐊᐱᖅᓱᑲᑕᓕᖅᑐᓂ ᐅᖃᐅᔾᔭᐅᒥᐊᒃᑲᓐᓂᕈᓐᓇᖅᑐᒥᓪᓗᓂ.

ᓯᕗᓪᓕᕐᒥ ᐊᖓᔪᖅᑳᖏᓐᓄ ᐊᐱᓕᓪᓗᓂ ᐊᒻᒪᓗ ᑕᑯᔅᓯᑎᓪᓗᓂᒋᑦ "head spin"-ᒥᒃ ᒧᒥᕐᓂᕐᒥᒃ.

ᐸᒃᑕᒃᑐᖅᑐᑎᒃ ᐊᒻᒪᓗ ᐸᑦᑕᒃᑐᖅᑐᑎᒃ--- ᑕᕝᕙ ᐋᓪᓚᒃᑐᓂ ᑕᖅᑲᑐᐊᕐᓂᑯᓗᑦ. ᐱᔭᕇᕈᓐᓇᕐᓇᓂᐅᒃ ᒧᒥᖅᑕᖓ.

"ᖃᓄᐃᓕᐅᖃᑦᑕᕋᐱᑦ?" ᐊᐱᕆᓪᓗᑎᒃ. "ᐱᕙᓐᓇᓂᖅᓴᐅᓛᕆᖅᐳᑎᑦ ᑭᖑᓪᓕᕐᒥᑦ."

Next he went to his grandparents. *Maybe they can help me,* he thought.

His grandfather was an expert drum dancer.

He danced an awesome "*hand stand*" for them and they were very impressed; but before the song ended, he fell down, too tired to finish.

They said, "What have you been doing? Better luck next time."

ᑭᖕᒍᓪᓕᕐᒥᑦ ᐃᑦᑐᑐᒃᑯᖕᒋᓐᓄᖅᑐᓂ. ᐃᑲᔪᕈᓐᓇᖅᐳᖅᑲᐃ ᐅᕙᓐᓂ, ᐃᓱᒪᓪᓗᓂ.

ᐃᑦᑐᖓ ᕿᓚᐅᔾᔭᒃᑲᒻᒪᓇᐊᓘᖕᒪᑦ.

ᒍᒥᑦᑎᐊᖅᑐᒻᒪᓇᐅᓪᓗᓂ "head stand"-ᒥ ᐱᐅᒋᔭᐅᔪᒻᒪᓇᐅᓪᓗᓂ---

ᑭᓯᐊᓂ ᓂᓪᓕᐊᔪᖅ ᐃᓱᓕᓚᐅᖅᑎᓐᓇᒍ, ᐋᓪᓚᒃᑭᓪᓗᓂ, ᑕᖅᑲᓗᐊᕐᓂᑯᒧᑦ ᐱᔭᕇᖅᓯᔭᕆᐊᖓ.

ᐅᖃᖅᑐᑎᒃ, "ᖃᓄᐃᓕᐅᖅᑲᑦᑕᕋᕕᓪᓕ? ᑭᖕᒍᓪᓕᕐᒥᑦ ᐱᔪᓐᓇᕐᓂᖅᓴᐅᓖᓕᖅᐳᑎᑦ."

ᓴᐱᓕᕐᑕᐃᓕᒥᑦ

Don't give up

Maybe my brothers and sisters can help me, he thought.

He rested for a few days then he called his six siblings together.

They clapped loudly as he danced "*free style*".

He was doing an amazing job for them—when suddenly, he fell down, too tired to finish.

They said, "What have you been doing? Better luck next time."

ᐃᓱᒪᓪᓗᓂ ᐊᖓᔪᑯᓗᒃᑲ ᐊᒻᒪᓗ ᓇᔭᑯᓗᒃᑲᖅᑲᐃ ᐃᑲᔪᕈᓐᓇᖅᑐᑦ, ᐃᓱᒪᓪᓗᓂ.

ᑕᖃᐃᖅᓯᑲᐃᓐᓇᓚᐅᖅᑐᓂ ᐅᓪᓗᓂᒃ ᖃᔅᓰᓇᓂᒃ ᑕᕝᕙᓂ ᐅᖄᓚᕕᒥᓪᓗᓂᒥᑦ ᐱᖕᒐᓲᔭᖅᑐᑦ ᖃᑕᙵᒍᑎᖕᒥᑦ ᐊᑕᐅᑦᑎᒃᑯᑦ.

ᐸᒃᑕᒃᑕᐅᕐᔪᐊᖅᑐᓂ ᒧᒥᖅᑎᓪᓗᒍ "free style"-ᒥᒃ ᒧᒥᑦᑎᐊᖅᑐᒻᒪᕆᐅᓪᓗᓂ ᑕᐃᒃᑯᓄᖕᒐ--- ᑕᕝᕙᓂ, ᐹᓪᓚᒃᑐᓂ, ᑕᖅᑲᓗᐊᕐᓂᑯᒧᑦ ᐱᔭᕇᕐᓇᓂ.

ᐅᖃᖅᑐᑎᒃ, "ᖃᓄᐃᓕᐅᖃᑦᑕᕋᕕᓪᓕ? ᑭᖑᓪᓕᕐᒥᑦ ᐱᔭᓐᓇᕐᓂᖅᓴᐅᓖᓕᖅᐳᑎᑦ!"

You Rule man
Be Cool Man
Be Cool
Hip Hop
Hip hop
Girl Power

A few days later, well rested, Isapee decided maybe he couldn't dance in front of his family.

So he asked eight of his teachers to meet him in the school gym to watch him dance.

Some of them even brought their video cameras. They cheered him on as he danced "*the back spin*".

They thought he was brilliant! He danced and danced until—all of a sudden, he fell down in front of them, too tired to finish.

He was so disappointed.

"What have you been doing?" they asked. "Better luck next time."

ᐅᓪᓗᖅ ᖃᐢᓯᒃᑭᐊᖅ ᐊᓂᒎᖅᑎᓪᓗᒥᑦ, ᑕᖃᐃᑦᑎᐊᖅᑐᓂ, ᐃᓯᒪᓕᖅᑐᓂ

ᒧᒥᖓᓇᖅᑐᓇᓂ ᖃᑕᙵᒧᑎᖏᑦ ᑕᑯᓈᖅᑎᓪᓗᒥᑦ.

ᐊᐱᕆᓪᓗᓗᓂᒋᑦ ᐱᖓᓲᔪᖅᑐ ᒪᕐᕉᓐᓂ ᐃᓕᓴᐃᔨᖏᑦ ᑲᑎᖃᑎᒋᔭᐅᕙᓪᓗᓂ

ᐃᓕᓐᓂᐊᕐᕕᐅᑉ ᐱᙵᒍᐊᕐᕕᖓᓂ ᑕᑯᓈᖅᑕᐅᓗᓂ ᒧᒥᖅᑎᓪᓗᒍ "back spin"-ᒥᑦ.

ᐱᐅᒋᔭᒻᒪᕆᐊᓘᓪᓗᓂ! ᒧᒥᖅᑐᓂ ᐊᒻᒪᓗ ᒧᒥᖅᑐᓂ ᑭᓯᐊᓂ---ᐹᓪᓚᑳᓪᓚᒃᑐᓂ

ᓯᕗᓂᖏᓐᓂ ᑖᒃᑯᐊ, ᑕᖅᓗᐊᕐᓂᑯᒧᑦ ᐱᔭᓈᓇᐊᖓ.

ᖁᕕᐊᓯᒍᓐᓃᖅᑐᐊᓘᓪᓗᓂ.

"ᖃᓄᐃᓕᐅᖅᑲᑦᑕᖁᕕᓪᓕ?" ᐊᐱᕆᓪᓗᑎᒃ. "ᑭᖑᓪᓕᕐᒥᑦ ᐱᔪᓐᓇᕐᓂᖅᓴᐅᓖᓕᖅᐳᑎᑦ."

What am I going to do? he thought. *I have to keep going. Maybe my friends can help me. They know me really well. I will ask them to watch me.*

Ten of his friends met him at the hamlet's C-hall and there he danced his heart out. "Go! Go! Go!" They shouted.

They cheered him on as he danced the "*popping*" dance.

Suddenly, without warning, he fell down exhausted. He couldn't finish.

He was so embarrassed.

"What have you been doing?" they asked. "Better luck next time."

ᖃᓄᐃᓕᐅᕐᓂᐊᓕᖅᐳᖓᓕ? ᐃᓱᒪᓪᓗᓂ. ᑲᔪᓰᓐᓇᕆᐊᖃᖅᑐᖓ. ᐱᖃᓐᓇᕆᔭᒃᑲᖃᐃ ᐃᑲᔪᕈᓐᓇᖅᑐᑦ ᐅᕙᓐᓂᒃ. ᖃᐅᔨᒪᑦᑎᐊᕐᒪᑕ ᐅᕙᓐᓂ. ᐊᐱᕆᓂᐊᓕᖅᐸᒃᑲ ᑕᑯᓐᓇᕐᑯᓗᒋᑦ ᐅᕙᓐᓂ.

ᖁᓕᑦ ᐱᖃᓐᓇᕆᔭᖕᒋᑦ ᑲᑎᖅᑎᕆᓪᓗᓂᒋᑦ ᐱᙳᐊᕐᕕᒻᒥ ᐊᒻᒪᓗ ᑕᐃᑲᓂ ᒧᒥᕕᐅᑎᑦᑎᐊᖕᒐᓂ ᒧᒥᖅᑐᓂ.

"ᐊᑏ! ᐊᑏ! ᐊᑏ!" ᖃᐃᒐᓪᓛᓪᓗᑎᒃ. ᖁᕕᐊᓯᔪᐅᓪᓗᓂ ᒧᒥᖅᑎᓪᓗᒍ "popping"-ᒥᑦ ᒧᒥᐅᓯᕐᒥᑦ.

ᑕᕝᕙᓕ, ᐃᓱᒪᑎᓐᓇᒍ, ᓵᓪᓚᒃᑐᓂ ᑕᖅᑦᑎᐊᖅᑐᓂ. ᐱᔭᓈᕈᓐᓇᐃᓕᓪᓗᓂ.

ᑲᙳᑎᑦᑐᐊᓘᓪᓗᓂ.

"ᖃᓄᐃᓕᐅᖅᑲᑦᑕᕐᕕᑦ?" ᐊᐱᕆᓪᓗᓂ. "ᑭᖑᓪᓕᕐᒥᑦ ᐱᔪᓐᓇᕐᓂᖅᓴᐅᓛᓕᖅᐳᑎᑦ!"

A week later, feeling sad but determined, he thought, *There's one more group I can dance for: the elders. They will know what the problem is.*

With determination, Isapee gathered twelve of them together, the best drum dancers in the hamlet.

He danced and danced and danced in front of them, the hardest dance of all, the "*spider walk*". They watched in amazement. Never had they seen a dance quite like this one before.

On and on he danced for the elders, as they watched this talented young man; but with the greatest of sadness, he fell down in front of the people he respected the most. He was too tired to finish.

They left the room one by one… all except his grandfather.

ᐱᓇᓱᐊᕈᓯᖅ ᓈᑎᓪᓗᒍ, ᖁᕕᐊᓱᑦᑎᐊᕐᓇᓂ ᑭᓯᐊᓂ ᐱᔪᓐᓇᑐᓇᓪᓗᓂ, ᐃᓱᒪᓪᓗᓂ: ᓱᓕ ᑲᑎᙵᔪᓄᑦ ᒧᒥᕈᓐᓇᖅᑐᖕᒐ. ᐃᓐᓇᑐᖃᕐᓄᑦ. ᖃᐅᔨᒪᓂᐊᖅᑐᑦ ᑭᓱᒥᑦ ᐊᑲᐅᙱᓕᐅᕈᑎᖃᕐᒪᖔᕐᒪ.

ᐱᔪᓐᓇᑦᑎᐊᖅᑐᕆᓪᓗᓂ, ᑲᑎᑎᑦᑐᓂᕆᑦ 12 ᐃᓐᓇᐃᑦ, ᕿᓚᐅᔾᔭᑲᐅᓛᑦ ᒧᒥᐅᓯᕐᓂᒃ ᒧᒥᖅᑐᓂᐅᒃ, "spider walk." ᑕᑯᓐᓈᖅᑐᑎᒃ ᓱᓕᔪᖅᓴᑦᑎᐊᖁᐃᔨᓇᑎᒃ. ᑕᐃᒫᒃ ᒧᒥᖅᑐᓂᒃ ᑕᑯᓚᐅᖅᓯᒪᙱᑦᑎᐊᖅᑐᑎᒃ.

ᒧᒦᓐᓇᖅᑐᓂ ᐃᓐᓇᑐᖃᕐᓄᑦ, ᑕᑯᓐᓈᖅᑕᐅᓪᓗᓂ ᒧᒥᒃᑲᒪᓇᐊᓗᖕᒥ ᐊᖑᒻᒥ... ᑭᓯᐊᓂ ᖁᕕᐊᓇᖕᒋᑦᑐᒥᒃ, ᐋᓪᓚᒃᑐᓂ ᓯᕗᓂᐊᓂ ᐱᖃᑎᒋᓂᖅᐹᖕᒋᑕ. ᑕᖅᔪᐊᓘᓪᓗᓂ ᐱᔭᕇᕐᓇᓂ.

ᐃᓪᓗᕈᓯᕐᒥ ᕿᒪᑏᑎᕙᓪᓕᐊᓪᓗᑎᒃ, ᐊᑕᐅᓯᐅᓈᖅᑎᖅᑐᑎᒃ... ᐊᑕᖕᒋᖅᑐᑎᒃ ᐃᑦᑐᖓᑕ ᐊᓯᖕᒋᑦ.

"Come," his grandfather said. "I know what the problem is."

"What? What is it? Please tell me, Grandfather," pleaded Isapee.

"I have been watching you, young man," said his grandfather. "You have to make a choice."

"What?" Please tell me!"

"You can't do both."

"Both? Both what?"

"You can't do drugs and dance. You must choose one, one or the other," his grandfather explained.

Isapee did not hesitate. "I choose dance!" he yelled.

"That's my boy, choose hip hope," his grandfather told him with pride.

"You mean 'hip hop', Grandfather," said Isapee.

"No, I mean hip hope...because I hope you will always choose dancing."

And from that day forward, Isapee began every dance with these words:

"Stop the drugs and start the Hip Hope!"

“ᖃᐃᓕᑦ,” ᐃᑦᑐᖓ ᐅᖃᖅᑐᓂ. “ᑭᓱᒥ ᐊᑲᐅᙱᓕᐅᕈᑎᖃᕐᒫᖔᖅᐱᑦ ᖃᐅᔨᔪᖓ.

“ᑭᓱ? ᑭᓱᒥᑦ? ᐅᖃᐅᑎᓚᐅᖓ, ᐃᑦᑑ,” ᐃᓴᐱ ᐅᖃᖅᑐᓂ.

“ᑕᑯᓐᓇᖃᑦᑕᕋᒃᑭᑦ, ᐊᖕᒍᑏ,” ᐃᑦᑐᖓ ᐅᖃᖅᑐᓂ. “ᓂᕈᐊᕆᐊᖃᕋᕕᑦ.”

“ᖃᓄᖅ? ᐅᖃᐅᑎᖓ!”

“ᑕᒪᒃᑭᓐᓂᐅᔭᓐᓇᖏᓐᓇᕕᑦ.”

“ᑕᒪᒃᑮᓐᓃ? ᑕᒪᒃᑮ ᖃᓄᖅ?”

“ᐋᖓᔫᕐᓇᖅᑐᖅᑐᑎᐅᓪᓗᑎᑦ ᒧᒥᖅᑎᐅᔭᓐᓇᖏᓐᓇᕕᑦ. ᓂᕈᐊᕆᐊᖃᕋᕕᑦ, ᓇᓕᐊᓐᓂᑐᐃᓐᓇᖅ,” ᐃᑦᑐᖓ ᐅᖃᖅᑐᓂ.

ᐃᓴᐱ ᓇᓗᖏᑦᑎᐊᖅᑐᓂ. “ᒧᒥᖅᑎᐅᔭᒪᔪᖓ!” ᖃᐃᒪᓪᓚᒃᑐᓂ.

“ᑖᓐᓇ ᐊᖕᒍᑎᕐᑯᑎᒐ, ᓂᕈᐊᕈᒃ “ᕼᐃᑉ ᕼᐆᑉ”, ᐃᑦᑐᖓᑕ ᐅᖃᐅᑎᓪᓗᓂᐅᒃ ᐅᐱᖃᓪᓗᓂ.

“ᐅᖃᖀᑦ “ᕼᐃᑉ ᕼᐋᑉᒦ,” ᐃᑦᑑ,” ᐃᓴᐱ ᐅᖃᖅᑐᓂ.

“ᐋᒃᑲ, ᐅᖃᖅᑐᖓ ᕼᐃᑉ ᕼᐅᑉᒥ”... ᓲᖃᐃᒻᒪ ᓂᕈᐊᖕᒍᔭᐃᓐᓇᖁᒋᒃᑭᑦ ᒧᒥᕐᓂᕐᒥᑦ.”

ᐊᒻᒪᓗ ᑕᐃᑲᖓᑦ ᐅᓪᓗᕐᒥᑦ, ᐃᓴᐱ ᐱᒋᐊᕈᑎᖃᐅᔭᐃᓐᓇᓕᖅᐳ ᒧᒥᓇᐊᓕᕌᖓᑦ ᐅᖃᖅᑐᓂ ᐃᒫᒃ:

“ᐊᖓᔫᕐᓇᖅᑐᑦ ᓄᖃᐅᑎᓗᒋᑦ ᐱᒋᐊᖔᓕᕆᑦ ᕼᐃᑉ ᕼᐅᑉᒥᑦ!”

DEDICATION

This story is based on a real hip hop dancer and is dedicated to all the b-boys and b-girls who dance away from drugs.

Thanks to our faith in Jesus Christ and our loving God who make ALL these things possible here in Clyde River!

Hip Hop Dancers
& Artists

Meeka Paniloo
& Buddha (CFM)

"Isapee"

Hip Hop Dancing
at the C-Hall

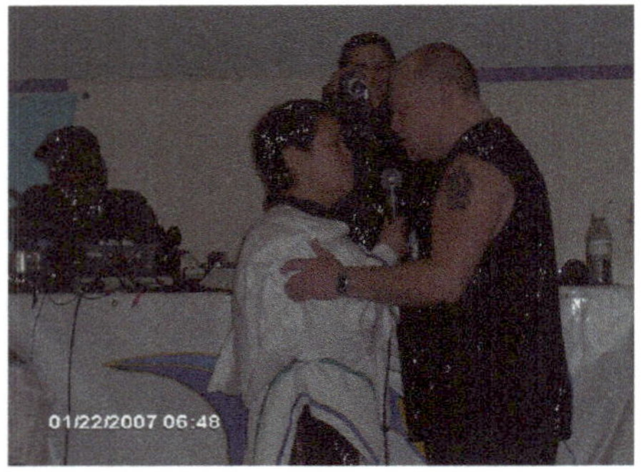

Throat Singing
& Beat-boxing

A Traditional
Inuit Drum

Dawn Elizabeth Doyle was born and educated in Toronto, Ontario. While teaching in nearby Orillia, her children traveled the world by ship. After their experience, they encouraged her to "get out there and see the world." Inspired by their sense of adventure and stories, she sold her house, and traveled to Mexico, the Middle East, Sri Lanka, Thailand, Japan, Egypt and Canada's Arctic.

While traveling and teaching, Dawn recorded, in words and pictures, the lives of the people she came to know intimately and respect deeply. These stories are first-hand accounts of living from sand to snow; tales she hopes to publish into a memoir now that she is retired from a 30-year career in national and international education.

It was during her last posting as a teacher in the North that her students came to her with their own story, one that they urgently wanted to tell the world: *The Hip Hope Dancer*. And so the tale begins, in the voices of Inuit children.

To see reviews, media and credentials, please visit Dawn's website: www.dawnofcomposition.vpweb.ca

www.ingramcontent.com/pod-product-compliance
Lightning Source LLC
Chambersburg PA
CBHW041203100726
47911CB00016B/846